An Inspirational Story About a Belov...
Journey Here on Earth and Bey...

O L I V E R ' S
S T O R Y

M.K. SAM QUANZ

Balboa Press books may be ordered through booksellers or by contacting:

Balboa Press
A Division of Hay House
1663 Liberty Drive
Bloomington, IN 47403
www.balboapress.com
1 (877) 407-4847

Because of the dynamic nature of the Internet, any web addresses or links contained in this book may have changed since publication and may no longer be valid. The views expressed in this work are solely those of the author and do not necessarily reflect the views of the publisher, and the publisher hereby disclaims any responsibility for them.

Any people depicted in stock imagery provided by Thinkstock are models, and such images are being used for illustrative purposes only.
Certain stock imagery © Thinkstock.

ISBN: 978-1-5043-7853-6 (sc)
ISBN: 978-1-5043-7854-3 (e)

Library of Congress Control Number: 2017905874

Print information available on the last page.

Balboa Press rev. date: 07/20/2017

BALBOA.
PRESS
A DIVISION OF HAY HOUSE

PROLOGUE

This is a little book about a little cockatiel with a big heart and an even bigger spirit. I began writing this story four days after he died because I had been given a profound sign that he had not just disappeared from the Universe. It was so empowering to me that I knew it was a story that must be shared.

I am a marketing consultant for a network television affiliate in Nebraska. I was out of town with nine associates when Oliver died and didn't know how I would get through all my appointments after I was told the devastating news.

The next morning I was in despair and asked God to show me a sign if Oliver was with Him. Then in typical fashion I began looking everywhere around me for anything that could be construed as a message direct from God to me. I was so sure I would see a cockatiel in a tree as I was driving. In Nebraska? Or perhaps a cloud shaped like his adorable little pointed head. I looked and listened with deadly focus as I drove to appointments and as I walked into offices that morning. As the warm spring day stretched toward noon, I became more depressed when I didn't see what I was looking for so desperately. Soon I began to fear that nothing was going to happen because *animals probably don't go to heaven.*

Then as so often happens when I get quiet and quit pushing for answers, it happened.

What I am about to share with you in this book is the peace and joy that God gave me that day. Losing a beloved friend, animal or human, is an incredibly painful experience, but there is such a reassuring peace in *knowing* we will see them again.

This is Oliver's Story, some of the highlights of our life together and the miracle I was given that made me understand he is NOT gone.

BIRDUMS

Oliver was a cockatiel parrot and was my constant companion and friend for twelve years. There was rarely a day that went by that he was not in my prayers. I believe the most important part of my prayers are to tell God of my gratitude for the blessings I have in my life; my children and grandchildren, my parents, my friends, my job, my health and Birdums. I never forgot what a gift he was.

His name was Oliver, but I called him Birdums when I talked to him. When speaking of him to others, I called him by his given name. My family and friends all knew him because he was almost always with me. He traveled with me when I could take him or he stayed with a friend who loved him such as Dave or Kay. Everyone who knew him was touched by him in some way. Not always in a positive way because not everyone likes birds but if you met him, you remembered him. My daughter Kym loved him very much but then she and her husband Tom have a cockatiel and understand what little rascals they can be. My daughter Jamie expressed her love for him to me after she found out he had died She remembered the first time he took food from her mouth. I know, yuck right? Shawn, Diann and Kristi, my other three children, more or less just put up with him because they knew how much he meant to me. Although why he meant so much to me might have been a mystery to them.

He was born in San Diego and was just twelve weeks old when I adopted him. He was with me though a separation and divorce and then a move from San Diego to a small town in the Midwest. I had been married for fifteen years and when that marriage was over I left San Diego to distance myself from him and memories and a career that was starting to take it's toll on me. I had to leave my grown daughters and and my new grandson Brock and move a thousand miles away - a very difficult thing to do but I needed a "new life" - away from a grueling escrow desk and the life squeezing stress that went with it. Because of this move, for many months, Oliver was my only friend and companion. I soon was busy building that new life and career in a new town. Oliver literally soaked up all this love and gave it back ten-fold. This little bundle of feathers made me laugh every day of our lives together.

The door to his condo (I never called it a cage for obvious reasons) was never closed unless he was outdoors with me while I mowed the lawn or sat in the glider on a beautiful day. When I was doing yard work, he was usually close by and would whistle and sing. When I was away from home, he always stayed inside his condo - I guess it was his security. Upon arriving home and coming through the door, I would hear "How's my Babe?" and he would come out to visit.

Oliver was a talker from an early age. First there were the easy things, a wolf whistle which every parrot picks up and kisses which are kiss noises. "How's my Babe" was his first phrase. He obviously picked this up from me because I always inquired about his day when I came through the door and asked that question of him. Birds are mimickers and collect their mimicked repertoire from phrases, songs and noises they here on a daily basis. Later he began to repeat "How's my pretty bird?" and "Peek a Boo" after I started to play that little game with him. Then there was "Here Kitty Kitty" that he picked up when he was about five or six. No, we didn't have a kitty, but I wanted to see if he could pick up new phrases at that age. That old saying "you can't teach an old dog new tricks" evidently didn't apply to cockatiels.

THE ROOSTER

Oliver did a rooster sound that was pretty hysterical. Because birds are mimicking the people they hear the sounds from, he picked up my idiosyncrasies. His cock-a-doodle-doo sounded a little like an old, cranky sick bird because he learned from - you guessed it - me! And that's how bad my rooster sounds. Before my move from San Diego I took Oliver on a commuter plane to San Francisco for a weekend with friends. His condo was in cargo and he was in a small pet carrier under the seat in front of me. As we were over Los Angeles he decided to do the rooster. The passengers hadn't really been aware that I was flying with a bird and I still remember the man in front of us turning around with questioning eyes and asked me "what do you have back there?" When I told him it was a cockatiel, he asked me if Oliver could come out so his little girl could see him. I took him out and set him on my knee and he entertained everyone with his entire repertoire - many how's my babes, beek-a-boos etc. Everyone, including the flight attendants thought he was a riot. I didn't worry about Oliver flying because I kept his flight feathers clipped.

THE WHISTLE GAME

One of Oliver's favorite games was the whistle game. He would start by whistling a few random notes and then wait for me to do the same random notes back. His rule - they must sound like his. Then when I did it correctly he would continue with another group of notes that was always just a little more complicated than the previous one. Each time I whistled back correctly he would come at me with one just a little more difficult. When I messed up, I received a loud squawk which was his equivalent of an admonishment that I just messed up big time. I always ended up laughing during his game because he was so funny as he squawked at me that I got it wrong and then would immediately continue with his string of "music" which continued to get louder and more difficult. This game always had the same end. Me laughing (and you can't really whistle when you're laughing) and Oliver giving up and preening because that is what birds do. Being a bird is a busy job.

BIRDIE MASSAGES

Because Oliver was hand-fed by humans from hatching to weaning, he loved to be near most people. He would step up on almost anyone's finger but he really didn't want to be touched. He was pretty cute so people usually wanted to "pet" him but he would open his beak and hiss at them usually discouraging any more direct contact. Beaks have a tendency to be sharp on the end, so people didn't engage further just in case he really wasn't kidding. He was about two years old before I earned his trust enough that he actually let me rub his head. But once he finally gave it a try, he realized this was what life was all about. Every night when I came home, he expected to have his head rub within a certain time frame. If I was busy and ignoring him, he squawked at me until I picked him up. The moment he stepped on my finger, he assumed the position. His little pointed head dipped down to let me know he was ready. Over time he would almost lie down in my hand as I rubbed his head his cheeks, under his chin and his neck. The only thing moving on his body was his head from side to side so I could reach the places that needed attention.

NO GREEN CARD

When Oliver was about three years old he became an "illegal alien". I actually had to smuggle my bird back in to the United States after a day of driving through Mexico. My ex husband Jim and I didn't plan ahead very well when we decided to leave California on a beautiful Sunday morning for a drive in the hills East of Tijuana Mexico. We left around ten in the morning with Oliver in the backseat in his condo. We drove for hours through small villages, stopping for lunch or to shop, sometimes just pulling to the side of the road to look out over a scenic valley. Around five on a lazy Sunday afternoon we arrived back at the San Ysidro border crossing to enter the US. After telling the border guard in Tijuana that we had nothing to declare, he coldly told us we could go on, but the bird would have to stay. I naively exclaimed, "Oh no sir, this is *my* bird. We brought him from San Diego with us this morning. We just went for a drive and are returning home." "That's fine, but as I said you can continue on, the bird stays. He will go to quarantine for six weeks!"

Well this news was handled with my usual finesse - I burst into tears. Jim, who was driving moved the car over into the "turnabout" and away we went back into Mexico. "Oh Jim, what are we going to do" I sobbed. There was no way I could leave Oliver in this third world country in quarantine. I was already entertaining thoughts of getting a job and living in Mexico with my bird. It actually seemed almost doable as Jim and I weren't going to actually make it together much longer anyway. But Jim, a former marine and ex-cop was street wise and imaginative and had other plans. We were going to drive back over the mountains to the Calexico border crossing and we would have to hide Oliver somewhere in the car before we got to the border and until we could get through.

Approximately two and half hours later we arrived at the Calexico border and stopped about a half mile from the line waiting to cross and pulled off on a side street. Jim removed the condo from the car and began dismantling it. Most of it was laid out flat and hidden behind the spare tire in the trunk. The line to cross into California was long and my Oliver sat on my leg preening. Being a bird is a busy job. As we approached closer, I emptied my purse to make room for a cockatiel. I became increasingly nervous as we approached the guard who stops each car, leans down with his head almost in the window and asks you what purchases you have to declare. I was literally shaking. I was positive the border guard at the Tijuana crossing had radioed our descriptions to this crossing and this was the end! *"Be on the lookout for a red Buick, license plate #____, two occupants and a bird trying to cross the border - shoot to kill!"* Oliver by this time was zipped into my bag and was by no means a happy camper. He was letting his feelings known. Loudly! We turned up the radio to try to drown him out and this made him furious and he squawked at a pitch that surprised even me. By the time we reached the border guard, I was nauseous and had a cold sweat all over my body. I waited for the guard to pull a weapon and order us to secondary inspection. But evidently the first border guard hadn't warned all the other crossings of the bird smugglers and this poor guy must have had really poor hearing because he motioned us through the gate and suddenly we were back in the good old USA and on our way home with a mere five hour delay because of taking Birdums to Mexico.

MOVED TO NEBRASKA
New Life, New Career and New friends

As I mentioned before, Birdums and I needed to find a new life. Suffice to say, my life was full of stress because of problems my husband had and couldn't deal with and unfortunately there was only one way to change that so I could be a whole person again. Leave California because leaving my husband meant I'd better find a place to live that wasn't so expensive if I was going to change my career at the same time. I moved to Grand Island Nebraska because it was close to where Mom lives in Kansas and we could see each other often with just a 2 hour drive. By the time a year had passed I had new people in my life and a job with a Television station that I absolutely loved.

Oliver was in birdie heaven when we had visitors and there were certain people he liked immediately and others that he decided he couldn't or perhaps just wouldn't trust. One of the latter was Dave. We dated for several months and Oliver just didn't like him. I am pretty certain that part of the reason he did't care for him is that Dave was always "in his face", constantly trying to get his attention, talking to him, chirping and whistling and trying to make friends. I told Dave on several occasions to just relax around him - even ignore him when he came in and Oliver would warm up. Dave just couldn't pull it off. He was so anxious for Oliver to like him he just pushed and pushed and the more he pushed the more Oliver would have nothing to do with him.

One afternoon, Dave came over to visit and was very excited by something that had happened that day and in his excitement of telling me about it he simply forgot about Oliver. We were sitting on the couch and Dave was telling me all about his excellent news. During this conversation (mostly Dave was talking and I was listening) I noticed Oliver climbing up the side of the couch right behind Dave. He stood about a foot behind him watching him talk to me. A few minutes went by and Oliver came closer. After a few more minutes he again moved closer to Dave but still without Dave noticing. Now I am keeping my eyes on Dave because I didn't want him swirling around if he noticed me looking at the bird, but in my peripheral vision I saw Oliver advance to the point he was perched on the couch cushion right behind Dave. Now being pretty talented at bird mind reading, I knew what Oliver was thinking - "what in the world is wrong with this guy tonight - he has never ignored me before and now he is over here only talking to mom - I don't get it and I don't like it!" With those thoughts it just finally was too much for a cockatiel to handle and he jumped on Dave's shoulder. The look on Dave's face was priceless. I told him softly not to move or look at him or talk to him for a little while and then to proceed slowly. Months of trying to coerce this little bundle of feathers into coming to him all to no avail and it had finally happened. It was the one thing Oliver just couldn't stand - being ignored!

BIRDS ON THE WIRE

Mu daughter Kym and her husband Tom adopted a cockatiel, most likely because they were so impressed by Oliver's antics. They named their baby Tyson and he is a very talented bird in his own right. I am always amazed at his musical abilities, he knows every bar of "Take Me Out to the Ballgame", "Pop Goes the Weasel" and "Jingle Bells". In fact he does them so unbelievably well that I used to think Kym was joking when we were talking on the phone and I could hear whistling in the background. The tunes were so perfectly in key that I was almost certain it had to be Tom, but Kym always insisted it wasn't, "Mom, it's Tyson, honestly!" His musical talent is really amazing. Oliver always tried to sing but unfortunately was always just a little off key.

On one of my visits from Nebraska to San Diego with Oliver, I spent three months at Kym and Tom's. Oliver and Tyson were forced to get to know one another. Actually it was Oliver who was forced. He really was completely bored with Tyson and it was obvious that he much preferred the company of people. Tyson on the other hand was absolutely mesmerized by his visiting "cousin". He was always leaving *his* condo and trying to enter Oliver's. If Oliver was in it at the time, he would immediately come out and leave Tyson's general vicinity. However in those three months together, Tyson picked up a little of Oliver's repertoire. He learned the Cock-a-doodle-do which of course sounded just like *me*.

When Oliver and I went back to Nebraska Kym and I were talking on the phone one day and Oliver was trying to get my attention at the same time Tyson was trying to get Kym's attention. Sometimes birds ignore you completely when you are trying to get them to show their talent to someone or you just want to hear one of their songs. But get on the phone and talk to someone else and they can't stand being ignored. We were laughing about how demanding our little guys were both being when we decided to see if they could hear each other on the phone. Well, not only did they hear each other, they began communicating with each other. They soon were whistling to each other, enjoying a long distance conversation over the phone wires. It was an amazing thing to witness.

TAP TAP TAP

I kept Oliver's blanket that covered his condo at night wrapped over the back of his condo during the day to provide a "back wall" where he could feel a little more secure or private when he needed it. When he was about six he discovered the cave it made where it draped on the floor and was quite often back there where he couldn't be seen, especially when I was away at work. I still remember the first time he found this place because when I came home from work that day I couldn't find him. I called and called him with no response - just silence. I hurried all over the house calling his name and becoming really scared when he didn't answer. I whistled until I couldn't whistle anymore and when he didn't reply to that in his usual way I started calling his name again. I really believe when he heard the fear in my voce as I searched for him, he decided he'd better let me know where he was. That is when I heard him tapping. He tapped his beak on the side of his condo and the second time I heard it, I knew where he was.

From that time on tapping became a new way of communicating where he was. Sometimes when I got home, I heard the old familiar "How's by Babe" coming from behind the blanket and sometimes I just heard "Tap Tap Tap". But he always let me know where he was. And when I got home, he didn't stay hidden very long. He always wanted to come out and be close to me until bed time.

THE TONGUE NOISE

My friend Kay spent many years around Oliver because she and I were together a lot. She and Birdums loved each other. There were times when she came to visit me after work when Oliver hadn't emerged from his cave yet, but when he heard Kay's voice he always came out to see her. In many ways pets are just like children and they sometimes get bored with their mommies and daddies and love when company shows up. Kay and her daughter Andra baby sat for Oliver on many occasions when I had to be out of town and couldn't take him with me.

When Oliver was about nine, he learned a new sound that was by far his very favorite. I made the sounds by "whirling" my tongue on the roof of my mouth while blowing through my teeth. He picked it up immediately and did this sound every day. In fact, when I couldn't get him to engage with any of his other repertoire this is the sound he just couldn't resist. It was the only sound he would always do on demand. I laughed when Kay told me about her inability to make this noise when she had been sitting for him one weekend. She said Oliver had been doing it incessantly and waiting for her to do it back and then squawking loudly at her when she didn't respond.

I showed Kay how I make the noise and she tried but just couldn't get it. Neither Oliver nor I could help her to learn it.

SOLO FLIGHT

When Oliver was only about one, before I left San Diego and moved to Nebraska, I almost lost him. Jim and I had taken him to the pet store to get his wings clipped because his flight feathers had grown. Evidently they had grown back completely and in our utter naivety, we got out of the car with him perched on Jim's shoulder. Bird Crazy where we adopted him is located just off the 15 Freeway in the Clairemont Mesa area of San Diego. When Jim stood up, Oliver took off in the clear blue sky of a warm San Diego afternoon. I watched in horror, as Birdums became just a speck in the sky with Jim sprinting off after him. Oliver flew off over the freeway arching in a circle to the South. Within seconds I lost sight of him as he disappeared behind a Denny's Restaurant.

There was soon a crowd of people in that parking lot looking up in the sky with us. Even some employees from Bird Crazy came out to see what was going on. I'm sure it was no more than 30 or 40 seconds, it seemed much longer, and my precious little bird appeared around the other side of Denny's and flew right back to the Bird Crazy store and perched on a cement precipice above the front door. To this day I still don't know if I had been screaming at the top of my lungs or if I had been shocked into total silence, but I hadn't moved from in front of the store while this all happened. An employee came out of the store with a ladder and I climbed up to Oliver and took him in my hands. I could feel his little heart pounding in his chest as we descended the ladder and went into the pet store. The manager of the store was looking at us in utter disbelief and said, "Do you know how lucky you are? No one EVER gets their bird back!"

While putting these little stories down on paper, I've realized that our life together started out with this miracle and our life together ended with another.

I THOUGHT HE WAS INJURED

The years passed and we were pretty much always constant companions. We were at our twelve year mark together and were in Kansas at my mom's house over the Memorial Day weekend. His condo was sitting on the kitchen counter where he could watch the birds playing in the bird bath outside. When I came out of the shower my mom told me Oliver had fallen off the counter. When I went to check on him he was visibly shaking and didn't seem to want to move so I assumed he was hurt from the fall. There are no Veterinarians who care for birds in this part of Kansas or Nebraska. Oliver's doctor was in Denver and that was six hours away so I watched him carefully throughout the day and by evening he seemed better. As I was holding him that evening I noticed an area on his neck that appeared swollen. The following morning he was back to his old self - climbing, talking, eating and preening. Over the next two weeks he seemed fine. The area on his neck, however, still seemed swollen and I decided to take him to Dr. LaBonde in Denver so he could check him over. Since our move from California to Nebraska, I had found an animal hospital in Denver that specialized in birds and reptiles. Oliver had been to see Dr. LaBonde several times over the years. Since he appeared to be doing fine I assumed he had dislocated his shoulder when he fell off the counter at my mom's house.

Mom and I left for Denver with Birdums over the weekend. We were going to visit my son Shawn and his wife Andee. They are the parents of my beautiful granddaughters, Mackenzie who was soon to turn two and Ashley her baby sister whom we hadn't met yet. Mom and I were anxious to see them and meet the new baby. I had made an appointment with Dr. LaBonde for Saturday morning to have Oliver's check up.

We took Andee and the girls shopping on Friday and out to lunch and had a wonderful dinner at Shawn's on Friday evening. We played with Mackenzie and held the new little one while we visited with their mom and dad. After several hours we said our goodbyes and returned to the hotel. Oliver had been in the hotel room for about 10 hours by himself and that is probably the reason for his unusual behavior when we got in. Birds typically roost (or nest) when the sun goes down and Oliver was no exception to that rule. He never -ever wanted to talk and engage in any activity late at night, but when I opened the room door and turned on the light he said "Hows my..". He stopped short of his usual question, "hows my babe?" I'm sure he was thinking - remember I can usually read his mind - Oops, this might not be mom, what if it's a stranger or a bear?" I laughed and said, "I'm fine, how's MY babe?" Reassured that no wild and unpredictable human or animal and entered the hotel room, he came out of his condo, snacked on some millet spray that I kept on top for him and then walked over to where I was sitting and perched on my foot until I reached down and picked him up. He assumed the position and got his birdie massage for about ten minutes. Then he sat on my knee and preened for a quarter of an hour. Remember, being a bird is a busy job. When he was tired of preening, he squawked to let me know he was ready to be inside his house and covered up for the night. I placed his cover over his condo and got into bed. We did a few "kiss noises" back and forth like we usually do at lights out and then we all went to sleep for the night, never knowing it would be our last together.

Our appointment with Dr. LaBonde was at ten the next morning. As we waited in the examination room for the doctor to come in, I experienced a premonition of what was about to take place. I just suddenly knew with certainty this was more serious than a dislocated shoulder. Dr LaBonde came in the room and we shook hands and talked a little about how I liked living in Nebraska and then he picked Oliver up and began feeling his neck. I held my breath as he turned to me at said, "Sam, this isn't an injury. This is a solid mass." Emotionally I was devastated, every fear I'd ever had about losing him was becoming real. "The only way I'll know what we're dealing with is to open it up" the doctor continued. "I do surgeries on Monday, so we'll find out then". The realization that I was going to have to leave Birdums and drive back to Nebraska without him began to dawn on me. But this Monday I simply had no choice. I HAD to be back to work on Monday because our entire sales staff was leaving Monday to go to Nebraska City for a sales blitz. I had set up about twenty appointments with business's there and I had to leave. And without a doubt, Oliver must stay. We had to find out what was happening inside his little body. And the only way to do that was surgery.

I remember walking outside and barely being able to see through the tears. I stood by my car and cried for a long time. And I began the first of many prayers concerning the operation he was about to endure. I asked God to be with him and Dr. LaBonde and to give me the strength to get through whatever was coming. When I got back to the hotel, Mom and I packed our things and started the long trip back home. We tried to stay upbeat - talking about how adorable the grand babies are and how wonderful it is that Shawn has found a beautiful loving wife. We were happy for them and I tried to concentrate on that as much as I could.

A DIFFICULT MONDAY

Monday morning came after a very long night. I was so worried about Birdums that I hadn't slept well and upon arriving in my office, I was watching the clock so I could call Homestead Animal Hospital and talk to the doctor. At 8:30, I made the call from my office. Dr. LaBonde told me he was going into surgery at 11:00 and that he would call me when it was over. I made some phone calls to some clients and tried to keep busy as the time slowly ticked away. The time in Denver is one hour earlier, so when I left for lunch, they were just starting the operation. I went home where I again asked God to be with Birdums and the doctor and nurses. I was scared and completely miserable that I wasn't in Denver with him.

The call came about 1:45. It was Dr LaBonde telling me that the operation was over. Oliver had a mass wrapped around his esophagus and it had been removed, necessitating a repair of 80% of his tiny windpipe. He told me Oliver was in recovery and very sleepy. Now we must just wait and see if there would be strictures in his esophagus, which would of course make swallowing/breathing difficult. Dr. LaBonde assured me he would call me with any changes and that I was welcome to call in whenever I wanted.

Once again I prayed, this time thanking Gd for being there with them and for the miracle of Oliver making it through surgery. When I got back into the office, I was feeling much better. I was just positive that everything was going to be fine. Birdums would heal, I'd go back to Denver and get him and life would be the same again.

NEBRASKA CITY

The next morning, my sales manager and I left Grand Island at 5:45 am. We had a two and a half hour drive to Nebraska City where we would be meeting the other sales associates for breakfast and two full days of appointments. After breakfast in a small cafe, I took off for my first appointment. I was in good spirits and breezed through my presentations and after the second was finished, I rushed to my car to call the hospital. I told the receptionist who I was and was put on hold for a couple of minutes. When Dr. LaBonde's voice came over the phone, I *knew*. "Sam, this is Dr. LaBonde. I answered "yes". The pause here seemed to last an eternity. "Oliver passed away about 7:30 this morning. We were checking him over and he began to cough. Probably the stress from coughing ruptured an incision and he began to hemorrhage and well...we just could not stop the bleeding...I am so sorry."

I think I may have said "okay". My mind had gone into that strange place that is referred to as shock. I remember thinking I felt totally numb. Dr. LaBonde then began telling me that I would need to decide what to do with his remains, that they work with a company that will cremate your pet either individually or with a group. I know he was speaking softly and kindly about this but to this day I still don't know exactly what was said between us. I must have told him I'd let him know and then I was off the phone and just sitting there in a parking lot in Nebraska City and feeling very alone.

The next hour is a blur in my memory. I know I went to another appointment, I don't remember many specifics about the meeting. I do remember telling each client that I lost a beloved pet that morning and they seemed to understand why I was not the usual upbeat sales person they may have been expecting. I also remember stopping to pray many times. I felt an overwhelming need to talk to God and thank him for letting me have my adorable and loving Birdums in my life for twelve years. I felt no anger, just an incredible sadness that our time together was over and I wanted God to know I understood that but needed His help to get through it.

My morning appointments were finished about eleven and I drove around Nebraska City until I found my friend Patti who is another sales associate working for the same television group. I followed her car for several blocks until she noticed me and pulled over. When we got out of our cars and were walking toward each other, I remember seeing her happy smile disappear as the look on my face registered with her. "Oh no" she said as she approached me. I'd told her at breakfast about Oliver's surgery so she just knew what had happened. Patti reached out and pulled me close to her and hugged me and I finally broke down. I cried and cried as his death finally hit me. Patti was finished with her morning appointments too so we got in her car and she drove. It was no accident that Patti was there for me that morning just like it was no accident that I had to be in Nebraska City when he had surgery, as I was soon to discover.

At noon we met our associates for lunch. I had pretty much gotten my head together or at least that is what I thought when I arrived. But as I sat there at our big table full of happy perky sales people all talking about their appointments and telling funny stories - it hit me again and I headed for the bathroom in tears. After several minutes I was again "in control" and went back to the table knowing I was going to have to offer an explanation of why I was an emotional mess. After I sat down and everyone was looking at me, I just blurted out "I lost my bird this morning and its going to be really rough because he was my buddy he talked to me and made me laugh every day of our lives together he said hows my babe when I walked in the door and gave me a wolf whistle when I got out of the shower and I need to talk about him"....whew - I finally took a breath! I then told my group of sales associates the stories - his flight on the commuter plane, his trip to Mexico and being smuggled back, his last night in the hotel when he thought a bear may have just entered the room and cut short his greeting to Hows my...! Everyone laughed, including myself at these tales of my little guy's life. I appreciated them listening and just talking about him helped me understand that my memories of him were the place I'd go to find the strength I'd need.

THE CEMETERY

That afternoon I was looking for a street address where I had an appointment later in the day and my drive took me past the cemetery. Nebraska City, a town in the South Eastern part of Nebraska is a beautiful little town. This is where Arbor Day originated so of course there are many trees beautifully planted along streets and around parks and businesses. History books are quite familiar with Nebraska City as this is where John Brown's Cave is located. It is now a museum where one can actually wander through the tunnels where the slaves were hidden deep in their caverns in the late 1800's while John Brown and his blessed group of sympathizers found ways to help them escape. As I passed along the outer perimeter of the cemetery I noticed the beautiful trees within. Shaded by these huge old trees is a cool stillness that lives there with the birds and squirrels. I have always found these old relics peaceful and fascinating. As I was driving along the street that surrounds it, a monument of an angel about 50 yards inside the gate caught my eye. Something about it seemed to beckon me and I thought of driving in to look, but talked myself out of it thinking to myself, you don't need to go in there - it will just make you sad which will make you cry again and you need to keep yourself together. I drove past and headed back toward Main Street to call on more potential customers.

STILL STRUGGLING

Somehow I managed to get through the day without completely falling apart, but can assure you that I did indeed come close that night in the restaurant where all of us met for dinner. The other sales associates were all from Lincoln which is only 30 miles from Nebraska City, so Clint and I were staying in a hotel there. We had gathered at a restaurant called Lazlos and I was tired and struggling to keep it together. I left the table twice and was in the ladies' room dabbing at tears that just wouldn't seem to stop sliding out of my eyes no matter how hard I tried to think of other things. One of the other women in our group had followed me in and when I turned and saw her standing there, she opened her arms to me and I just fell into them like a small child who needed comforting. She held me while I sobbed. I cried and cried and cried and she just held me in her arms and told me how sorry she was and how she understood how unbearable it can be to lose a beloved pet. I needed that cry and I really needed her at that time of letting go. I will always treasure that hug from her!

After dinner everyone moved from the restaurant to the bar to have a drink and tell war stories and laugh and loosen up. I need to shut down mentally so I went to the hotel and went to bed early. I slept long and hard and when my alarm went off at 6:30 I hit the shower and was in my car and on the road again in just over an hour. On the 30 minute drive back to Nebraska City I had time for prayers on the way. I'm a good driver. My eyes are always on the road and who is around me, but that doesn't stop me from talking to God. I've always found driving to be a perfect place to commune with Him. Maybe not on the I-5 from Oceanside to San Diego in rush hour traffic, but then, this is Nebraska not California.

ASK AND YOU SHALL RECEIVE

I always knew when Oliver left me my heart would break. What I didn't now beforehand and didn't have the opportunity to comprehend until the day after he died, was that he didn't just disappear. In the midst of my utter despair I asked God to give me a sign if Oliver was with Him and the sign I was given reached beyond anything I could have imagined. It brought me immediate peace with the knowledge that our beloved pets are also part of this incredible universe and afterlife.

After finishing all my morning appointments, I decided to look for the business I was seeing first thing that afternoon. That way upon finishing lunch, the drive there would be easy and stress free. The drive took me past that cemetery I had seen the day before and again I felt compelled to go in when I saw that Angel from the street. I shook off the feeling and continued around the circle drive, intent upon finding the business I was looking for. Several minutes later I found the street I'd been seeking and then located the business. Yes, now I knew exactly how to get there after lunch. On the return trip back around the cemetery, this time I turned in when I saw that Angel. She was about fifty yards along the stone driveway and I stopped when I was half way there and shut off the engine and rolled down the windows. The day was really heating up but inside this cemetery under these huge old trees, it must have easily been close to 15 degrees cooler. I walked along the drive way looking at this huge stone Angel's face and wondering why she was calling me. She was lovely and seemed to exude serenity. She seemed to be a harbinger of peace and joy for all eternity as she silently watched over someone's final resting place forever. I stood there looking up at her - waiting.... and nothing happened. No sign from her or from anywhere. No little cockatiel perched on her wing.....nothing. I was suddenly quite sure there would be no sign from her. I just felt confused as to why I felt so compelled to enter here each time I saw her. I probably just needed to take in the peacefulness of my surroundings and that was most likely why I'd felt this strong need to come in.

I turned around and just began to take in the beauty of the stones and markers and trees and flowers in this beautiful place. As I looked around I noticed a very striking monument a little distance away. It was a perfectly round granite sphere that was probably 5 or perhaps even 6 feet in diameter. I began approaching it to get a closer look because it's unique shape was intriguing. As I walked around it I saw the name of Mason inscribed on it as the family's surname. I noticed three wedge shaped granite markers on the other side of it and walked around to look at them. The first name I saw litteraly made me gasp - it was 'OLIVER'. Emotions rushed through me as I fell to my knees and began to weep. I had asked God for a sign if Oliver was with him. I traced each letter with my finger - O-L-I-V-E-R. Time disappeared, perhaps I was there on the ground for 15 minutes, I'm not sure. But I cried for my lost companion. He had been with me for over a decade, with me during a painfull divorce and with me as I moved far from my family and friends in San Diego to a town where I knew no one and he was the one I came home to at night. He was the one that talked to me when I felt low and made me laugh. And now he was gone. I felt the emptiness of what it would feel like when I got back home after this business trip and no one said "hows my babe" when I walked in the door. Knowing he had died and I hadn't been with him. All the pain from these thoughts rushed into my heart and I felt desolate and lost. I began to question why God had brought me here to see my little Birdum's name on this grave marker. It just made me incredibly sad. What was the point?

As I'd been sitting there on the grass, I hadn't paid any attention to the other two markers beside Oliver's. As I wiped tears from my eyes, I noticed the first one beside Oliver and the name was Perry - my grandfather's name. My mother's father. I knew Perry had been his name (he had died before I was born) and that seemed to register slightly in my grieving sub-consious and I ran my fingers over Oliver's name once more and began to rise off the ground so I could pull myself together and leave, again wondering if God was trying to tell me something, but deciding I was just trying to force something. That was when I saw the third stone and the engraving on that stone was Mary. Oh my God in heaven. It seemed to hit me like a bolt of lightning. Mary was Perry's wife here in this cemetery - side by side for all eternity with their son Oliver. Mary was also my Grandmother's name - Perry and Mary were my grandparents. I had never met them, but I knew how much my mother loved them. She still does. She talks about them with complete love and devotion that has never wained in her more than 50 years since they have been gone. My grandparents are buried side by side in Phillipsburg Kansas and I have gone to the cemetery countless times over the years with my mom to put flowers on their graves. I have stood there and gazed at those names Perry and Mary and wondered what they were like. And now here I am in this cemetery in a little town far from home and and looking at those three names Perry, Mary and Oliver and now I know why I was called here. I now knew with my heart and soul, that this was the miracle I'd prayed for. I'd asked for a sign if Oliver was with Him and this was God's perfect gift to me. It was if I could hear my very own grandparents whispering in the wind out there in that beautiful and peaceful, cemetery, "He's okay, he's with us."

An incredible peace came over me as I realized what had just been given to me. My little feathered friend was gone from me, but he was not gone from the Universe. He had just moved on to another place. Like my grandparents and my Dad, like all of us must and all of us will. This answered prayer was so empowering. It absolutely confirmed my belief that there is life after life for us. What absolute joy I felt in the midst of my grieving. I have always believed we simply passed into another realm of existence upon our death and now with the knowledge that came from this miracle I now know something more, our beloved pets do the same.

As time goes by and the pain of my loss becomes a little less each day, I am still filled with incredible awe when I think of that day. I was 200 miles from home when Oliver died. I had never been to Nebraska City before and yet within an hour of finding out that Oliver was gone, a stone angel was calling me into a cemetery where I would find a miracle when I needed it most.

Because I'm in sales, I'm in my car a lot and I still talk to God when I drive. I have a little Angel dangling from my rear view mirror. She is there to remind me to thank Him for all that is good in my life and to ask for his divine guidance each day.

Birdums continues to be in my prayers. I thank God for giving us twelve years together. I still miss him, but I miss him with joy in my heart because he is still here in the Universe. I know, because my grandparents whispered to me that day, "He's okay, he's with us".

CPSIA information can be obtained
at www.ICGtesting.com
Printed in the USA
LVOW06s2358060817
544058LV00052B/391/P

9 781504 378536